TWENTIETH-CENTURY DEVELOPMENTS IN FASHION AND COSTUME

MEN'S COSTUMES

Other books in this series include:

Military Uniforms

Carol Harris and Mike Brown

Accessories

Carol Harris and Mike Brown

Children's Costumes

Carol Harris and Mike Brown

Women's Costumes

Carol Harris and Mike Brown

Festivals

Ellen Galford

North American Dress

Dr. Louise Aikman

Ceremonial Costumes

Lewis Lyons

The Performing Arts

Alycen Mitchell

Everyday Dress

Chris McNab

Rescue Services

Carol Harris and Mike Brown

Religious Costumes

Ellen Galford

Introduction

Every day we go to our closets with the same question in mind: what shall I wear today? Clothing can convey status, wealth, occupation, religion, sexual orientation, and social, political, and moral values. The clothes we wear affect how we are perceived and also reflect what image we want to project.

Fashion has always been influenced by the events, people, and places that shape society. The 20th century was a period of radical change, encompassing two world wars, suffrage, a worldwide Depression, the invention of "talkies" and the rise of Hollywood, the birth of the teenager, the global spread of television, and, later, the World Wide Web, to name just a few important developments. Politically, economically, technologically, and socially, the world was changing at a fast and furious pace. Fashion, directly influenced by all these factors, changed with them, leaving each period with its fashion icon.

The 1920s saw the flapper reign supreme, with her short dress and cropped, boyish hair. The '30s and '40s brought a wartime mindset: women entered the workforce en masse and traded their silk stockings for nylon. During the conservative 1950s—typified by twin sets and capri pants—a young Elvis Presley took the world by storm. The '60s gave us PVC, miniskirts, and mods, and in 1967, the Summer of Love spawned a new language of fashion in which bell-bottoms and tie-dyed shirts became political expressions of peace and love. In the 1980s, power and affluence became the hallmarks of a new social group, the yuppies. Designer branding led the way, and the slogan "Nothing comes between me and my Calvins" started an era of status dressing. The 1990s will be best remembered for a new fashion word introduced by the underground street and music movement of Seattle, grunge.

Twentieth-Century Developments in Fashion and Culture is a 12-volume, illustrated series that looks at changing fashions throughout this eventful century, and encourages readers to question what the clothes they wear reveal about themselves and the world they live in.

Special introduction and consultation:
JONES NEW YORK

CHAPTER 1

All Suited Up: 1900–1940s

In fashion terms, the beginning of the 20th century marked one of the most radical changes in menswear: the growing popularity of the modern suit. Toward the end of the 19th century, informal suits, called "lounge suits," and business suits became the uniform of the middle classes.

Suit jackets were cut straight, with wide shoulders and narrow lapels, and were fastened high in the front, with four buttons. Business suits also had a small, flat pocket

Clark Gable (left) was a 1930s' icon for the all-American male. Gertrude Lawrence and Ivor Novello (right), two British theater stars well-known in the United States, epitomize 1930s' sophistication.

designed to hold a subway or bus ticket, a sign that large numbers of the growing middle class were living in newly built suburbs and traveling daily to the city to work. Vests were plain, dark in color, and fitted; they were made from wool or wool mixtures. Suit pants were narrow and, in the early part of the century, had no cuffs.

INTERNATIONAL SUIT STYLE

The suit was popular in both the United States and across Europe, although U.S. versions were noticeably more colorful and less formal. Thanks to the huge variety of clothing styles among the immigrant communities and the need for durable and practical clothing, great ranges in style were available. Unlike their European counterparts, even gentlemen in the U.S. wore clothes that were cut for comfort and easy movement.

THE ARISTOCRATS

London was the center for men's clothing, and in many ways, the equivalent to Paris for ladies' fashions. While most men wore clothes that had little to do with fashion, there were a few exceptions: the extremely wealthy "men about town," including the Prince of Wales (later known as King Edward VII) and his continental companions, the Marquis de Castellane-Novejean and Prince de Sagan. However, these aristocrats set trends only within their own social group, and the styles they wore had little influence on those outside of their class.

LOOSER STYLES

By the time King Edward VII died, in 1910, several changes had been made to the **single-breasted** suit. Tailors introduced high, shaped waists and sloping shoulders to jackets, which now had only three buttons. Pants had cuffs and were cut deliberately above the ankles. European men wore American-style boots and shoes.

From 1925 onward, **double-breasted** suits became as popular as single-breasted styles. Bright colors and **checks** were worn alongside brightly colored **Fair Isle** knitwear, striped blazers, white flannel pants, and **tweed** jackets. Despite the less-formal attitude toward clothes, however, men always wore hats—even just striped cricket caps—to match their blazers.

Looser pant styles meant that underwear became looser as well. Combined undershirts and long underpants known as **long johns**, which were made from fine wool, were still popular, but now health-conscious people thought cotton or silk boxer shorts more hygienic.

HEADGEAR

At the beginning of the 20th century, hats were essential fashion items and were worn by men of all classes at all times. Cloth caps were working-class headgear, and were worn mainly at work. King Edward VII introduced **Homburg hats** as leisurewear; they only became formal city headgear when worn 20 years later in a fashion started by the British Foreign Secretary of the time, the dapper Anthony Eden. Both men and women, while engaging in leisurely activities on the river, wore straw

In the 1999 film *Gods and Monsters*, Ian McKellen played the film actor and director James Whale, here wearing a typical 1930s-style three piece suit, topped with a stylish fedora.

BROOKS BROTHERS

One of the first stores to sell ready-to-wear clothing for men, Brooks Brothers opened in New York in 1818 as the Brooks Clothing Company, changing its name to Brooks Brothers in 1850. The company popularized many of the styles that are still standard components of most men's wardrobes today. Shirts with button-down collars (originally worn in England by polo players) were introduced in 1900, followed by other fashions inspired by British menswear, such as garments made from Harris tweed and Shetland sweaters. Throughout the 20th century, Brooks Brothers' understated, informal style has rarely been out of fashion. Today, it is associated especially with the styles of clothing worn by students at Ivy League universities.

boaters, popular since the 1880s. **Panama hats** had also been around for a while, dating back to 1855, when Emperor Napoleon III of France introduced them to Europe. This tightly woven straw hat, originating from Ecuador, was a luxurious dress item for the summer. In 1906, Theodore Roosevelt wore one on a trip to the Panama Canal, setting a trend among American men.

SHOES

American-style shoes were more comfortable for walking than the British or

These early 20th-century brogues can be identified as American by the rounded toes and soles wider than the uppers.

European versions, which were made with horseback riding in mind. The American styles had round (rather than pointed) toes, soles that were wider than the uppers, slightly raised heels, and wide laces. Some shoes were decorated with holes punched in the leather; these were called brogues.

THE DANDY

At this time, the general trend was toward more comfortable clothes in sober colors, rejecting the decorative—and now outdated—look of the leisured classes. The Edwardian dandy was, however, an exception to this rule. A well-off and less-conventional member of the middle class, the dandy might wear a brightly colored or intricately patterned vest, carry a cane, and wear a **cravat** in place of a tie. He might also wear a striped shirt in **taffeta** or silk instead of the usual cotton or wool. Men who wished to be thought especially fashionable would wear a Chesterfield coat, a closely fitted, single-breasted overcoat with a velvet collar. This style of coat went in and out of fashion throughout the 20th century.

THE PRINCE OF WALES

For most of his adult life and until his death in 1910, the Prince of Wales was the best-known, most-stylishly dressed man in the Western world. His outfits were seen during his public forays, when he visited all of the most fashionable European resorts, went shooting on his estate, or attended the horse races. His clothing was the subject of endless comment in both the European and American presses. Trends set by the Prince include those for Homburg hats, **Tyrolean hats**, creases down the front of pants (initially from the knee downward), pant cuffs, **spats**, unbuttoning the lowest vest button, ties, cravats, and walking canes.

A QUIETER STYLE

As the world drifted toward war, King George V—who had by now succeeded his father, King Edward VII—inadvertently encouraged a more sober approach to dress. George made a virtue out of his old-fashioned, more formal clothes. In contrast to his father, he had no interest in fashion. At the same time—and as was the case with women's clothing—more radical forces were making an impact on dress. In France, Italy, and Russia, artistic movements, such as the Post-Impressionists, the Futurists, and the Constructivists, produced textiles and clothing that rejected the formality of the suit. Although these movements contributed colorful and entertaining styles, most men preferred quieter and more restrained styles of dress.

MILITARY STYLE

Like every major international conflict, World War I had a huge impact on social customs, including dress. Military styling was popular at this time, and men bought all of their clothes—civilian and military, bespoke (made-to-measure) and ready-to-wear—from the same places. A typical advertisement from this time, from the Kahn Tailoring Company of Indianapolis, covered all of the purchasing possibilities with its slogan, "The Kind of Clothes Gentlemen Wear," and claimed it had "An Authorized Representative in your City and at Every Camp."

THE TAILORING INDUSTRY

In the early part of the 20th century, London's Savile Row—a street widely considered to be the home of bespoke men's tailoring—had plenty of work from well-to-do customers from both the United States and Europe. Outside of London (and its social scene), however, mass-production techniques began taking over the tailoring industry in the U.S. and Britain. Bespoke tailor shops began facing stiff competition from factories in which garments were produced "off-the-rack" using the latest American mass-production techniques. These techniques

ARROW SHIRTS

A New York-based firm, Arrow became well known in 1913 for a range of advertisements that featured sporty men in Arrow collars and shirts. By the end of World War I, in 1918, the company was producing 400 different types of collars. In the 1920s, it created a shirt with an attached collar, as well as a range of tailored shirts. After World War II, it developed a wide range of colored shirts. The company also promoted a range of womenswear based on its shirt designs for men.

benefited from sewing machines, cutting machinery, and different approaches to manufacturing in factories. In the meantime, toward the end of the 19th and the beginning of the 20th centuries, the **pogroms** in Russia encouraged an upsurge in immigration from Russian Jews, many of whom, like other European Jews, were tailors by trade. The American tailoring industry also benefited from the new approaches this particular group of refugees brought with them.

ANDROGYNY

The end of World War I left millions in the U.S. and Europe mourning what was known as the "Lost Generation": the millions of young men who had fallen on the battlefields. This lack of young men encouraged the onset of a new fashionable look for both young men and young women: the boyish young man, or Ganymede, Zeus' beautiful male cupbearer from classical Greek mythology. Because of this fashion trend, many young people looked sexually ambiguous throughout the 1920s.

ANOTHER ROYAL FASHION ICON

As the 1920s began, Edward, Prince of Wales and grandson of the late King Edward VII (another male fashion icon), arrived. Like his grandfather, he was known for his strong commitment to relaxing in fashionable resorts around the world and for wearing the latest styles. His playboy lifestyle, which involved running around with beautiful women (both married and single), was enthusiastically recorded in American magazines of the time, especially as his relationship with the twice-divorced American, Mrs. Wallis Simpson, grew.

OXFORD BAGS

The British press regularly blacked out images of the Prince's scandalous affair with Wallis Simpson, and American magazines were sold with pages and photographs removed, yet the Prince's personal style was still followed closely. One of his earliest contributions to fashion was to make **Oxford bags** popular. These were straight-cut pants with wide legs originally 28 inches (71 cm) in diameter, but getting wider and wider, much to the amusement of onlookers.

RENEGADE ROYAL STYLE

Not only was the Prince of Wales an ambassador for British textiles and fashions, he also promoted the easier and more relaxed fashions of the American menswear trade. In fact, his London tailors were shocked that he had his pants made in New York and that he wore them in the American style: with a belt rather than suspenders.

rather than an essential, part of the male wardrobe. Designers Ted Lapidus and Yves Saint Laurent created the popular safari suit, so called because it drew on the style worn by big game hunters and photographers on safari, made from light-colored materials and with patched, pleated pockets.

MUSICAL INFLUENCES

The styles of popular musicians dominated men's fashion during the 1960s. One particularly influential figure was Bob Dylan, a musician who had taken folk singing to a wider audience, beyond the specialist clubs. The styles he wore were typical of folk and protest singers of the time, but as he entered the pop charts, other musicians, such as John Lennon, Janis Joplin, and Donavan, imitated his style, espeically his trademark floppy cap. Dylan remained influential throughout this decade, both for his political protest songs and for his clothes, although both veered away from the styles linked with traditional folk music.

The safari clothes shown here in the 1965 film *Born Free* inspired designers to create the safari suit.

ANDY WARHOL ON BOB DYLAN, 1965

"At Sam's party, Dylan was in blue jeans and high-heeled boots and a sports jacket, and his hair was sort of long. He had deep circles under his eyes and even when he was standing, he was all hunched in. He was around 24 then, and the kids were all just starting to talk and act and dress and swagger like he did. But not many people except Dylan could ever pull that anti-act off—and if he wasn't in the right mood, he couldn't either. He was already slightly flashy when I met him, definitely not folksy any more—I mean, he was wearing satin polka-dot shirts."

—Andy Warhol and Pat Hackett, *POPism: The Warhol '60s,* 1981

In 1967, the Beatles' album, *Sergeant Pepper's Lonely Hearts Club Band,* set the trend for old-fashioned, military-style jackets. The Beatles, who traveled to India, were also enormously influential in encouraging the vogue among hippies for Eastern—especially Indian and Nepalese—styles and textiles.

HIPPIE STYLE

The hippie movement, or counterculture, was a reaction against the consumer values of the post-war era. It also grew out of the massive civil rights protests that were sweeping across the United States and out of protests against the Vietnam War. Protest songs and liberal politics, art, and music were all part of a movement that rejected the values and aspirations of the previous generation.

The hippies, together with a more radical element, the yippies (Youth International Party members), all wore distinct clothing that was symbolic of their anti-consumer values. Secondhand and homemade clothes were popular as part of the new fashion for crafts. Another, ironic fashion for the peace protesters was U.S. Army surplus clothing. The peace movement also appropriated the "Stars and Stripes" pattern for a t-shirt. In the 1990s, the followers of grunge music carried on the hippies' anti-consumerist ideas, creating their own style based around secondhand clothes bought in thrift shops and flea markets.

1970s COUNTERCULTURE

In the 1970s, the fashions of the counterculture became mainstream styles for younger men. Sexual liberation, especially the repeal of laws that, in many countries, had outlawed homosexuality, also encouraged a more flamboyant approach to dressing.

In musical terms, "glam rock" was the label given to artists whose sexuality was ambiguous and who dressed in glittering and glamorous clothes. Even the most committed heterosexual men were influenced by glam rock and started wearing eye shadow and lip gloss, sometimes in conjunction with stubble on their faces. The musician Lou Reed and the rock group The New York Dolls, whose members were dressed like transvestites, represented one extreme of this fashion trend in the United States, while David Bowie was the bisexual leader of the fashion pack in Europe. Other musical acts, such as Roxy Music, wore fashions based on the 1930s' "lounge lizards" look, a successor to the 1920s' "gigolo" look.

The hippie style of the late 1960s drew inspiration from ethnic-based costumes, crafts, and thrift shops.

33

EXAGGERATION

In the 1970s, men's fashions were all about exaggeration. Pants were flared, and the straight cut of the Oxford bags of the 1920s was back. This time, however, pants were worn with stacked heels or platform shoes, adding a few extra inches in height. Shirts were now shorter in the body, and pants were high and closely fitted at the waist. Cuffs on sleeves were pointed and jacket lapels were very wide.

STREETWEAR

In France, the designer Yves Saint Laurent announced that for both men and women, fashion was now inspired by styles worn on the street, rather than the other way around. Suits were still available in the traditional made-to-measure way, but the younger generation was far more likely to buy its clothes from ready-to-wear shops—and to wear a jacket and pants that did not necessarily match. This trend for mismatched clothing was taken to an extreme in the fashion for wearing wildly clashing colors, patterns, and fabrics.

UNISEX STYLES

Based primarily on men's fashions, unisex styles emerged during the 1960s, and from the late 1960s onward, vests were a popular part of this trend. They were typically worn unbuttoned, with jeans, and were

David Bowie led the glam look in England, often wearing elaborate face makeup and flamboyant androgynous clothing.

often heavily decorated and embroidered. This new style for vests owed a lot to the increasingly popular fashion for clothes that had their origins in the traditional styles of various ethnic groups. The peasant look, another popular style of the time, was a version of this trend, and drew on the traditional cultures of Eastern European and other Eastern ethnic groups. Another popular, ethnically inspired unisex item was the Afghan coat, a rough, heavily embroidered coat made from goatskins.

The pullover, a sleeveless sweater in the 1920s, also came back into fashion at this time. Influenced by military styling, the 1970s versions were multi-colored, with round (rather than V-shaped) necks. These garments were known as **tank tops**, because they were modeled on the styles worn by tank crews in the military.

DENIM

Patched and faded, denim was everywhere in the 1970s. Typically used to make widely flared pants, it was also used for jackets, shoulder bags, hats, and shoes. By 1976, Levi-Strauss, who had originally designed his denim jeans as workwear, was the largest clothing manufacturer in the world. As jeans became an acceptable form of casualwear for men of all ages, designer-label jeans made their first appearance. Calvin Klein was the first name on designer jeans. Armani followed this trend; his jeans were generally worn by the younger generation.

PUNK STYLE

Punk rockers appeared in the mid-1970s, first in Britain, and then quickly becoming popular with teenagers across the U.S. As with glam rock, bad taste was a feature of punk; punk rockers did all they could to shock the established order. The punk look took conventional clothes, such as suits and blazers, and ripped them apart, then decorated them with razor blades, Nazi regalia, chains, and safety pins. Bondage pants, in which the legs were tied together loosely, were a preferred style. Other references to sadomasochistic sex were seen in the use of spiked dog collars and rubber and PVC (polyvinyl chloride) garments. The black plastic garbage bag was the basis for many items of punk clothing, because it was one of the cheapest and most commonplace materials. Designer Vivienne Westwood, whose shop on London's King's Road became the center for the latest fashions, was a leader in punk fashion.

THE NEW ROMANTICS

Glam rock continued to influence style into the 1970s, drawing on the clothes traditionally worn by pirates, 18th-century highwaymen, and Native Americans. At the beginning of the 1980s, this style was reinvented as the "new romantic" movement. Inspired by the dandies and fops of England in the late 18th century, the new romantics wore heavy eye makeup, and they dyed their hair jet black, then gelled it into spiky points in a style reminiscent of that of the punk rockers.

Some, known as "goths," wore eyeliner and dark lipstick, creating a gothic version of the move-ment. Typical attire included heavily

Stiff, lacquered hair was too dramatic a fashion statement to disappear with 1970s' punk rockers. In the 1980s, the new romantics and the goths continued the hairstyle.

THE CASUAL YEARS: 1950–1990s

THE MOHAWK

Many punks, especially males, wore their hair in a "Mohican" style, named after the Native American tribe. To create this style, which came to be known as a "Mohawk," the head was shaved—with the exception of a narrow center band of hair that ran from the front of the head to the back. This center growth was often worn long, bleached, dyed in unnatural colors, and stiffly lacquered so that it stood up several inches from the head.

---

decorated jackets, narrow drainpipe pants, and shirts with ruffles down the front and frills at the cuffs.

THE MAN ON THE STREET

As exciting and influential as the punk and new romantic styles were, they never became part of male mainstream fashion. Most men found that in the workplace, something less aggressive was required. Stylish and inexpensive suits, particularly in wool mixtures, were made to meet the demands of ready-to-wear fashion. In the late 1970s, these suits were produced primarily in Italy. By the end of the decade, however, all of the major designers had created their own menswear labels. In the early 1980s, Giorgio Armani, Hugo Boss, and Nino Cerrutti were the most popular labels on ready-to-wear suits.

A RETURN TO FORMALITY

At the beginning of the 1980s, mainstream fashion was becoming increasingly concerned with fashionable and sober styling, much of it American-led. The spur for this dress trend was the election of Ronald Reagan, who replaced Jimmy Carter as president of the United States. In deliberate contrast to the casual jeans and working-shirt style of Carter, Reagan wanted more formality

Military styling, and camouflage patterns in particular, were popular styles for the second half of the 20th century.

at the White House. One of his first acts as president was to order military personnel in Washington back into full uniform.

GREED IS GOOD

The United States was relatively prosperous in the 1980s, and wealth was something to be flaunted. The term yuppie (derived from the phrase "young, upwardly mobile professionals") was widely used to describe young working people who were earning huge salaries and usually making a virtue of their amoral approach to profit. Vests, especially in eye-catching styles and prints, were now back in fashion, as were brightly contrasting ties and suspenders. In the 1987 film *Wall Street,* the actor Michael Douglas, playing the financier Gordon Gecko, summed up this look with his red suspenders, worn with a colored shirt and a white collar. His character's announcement that "greed is good" summed up the general climate of this decade.

GAY FASHION

Having been brought out into the open by the sexual liberation movement, gays in the 1980s became role models for mainstream fashion, and their clothing styles were copied by men everywhere. The "clone" style—which consisted of a white t-shirt worn with stylish jeans, a full moustache, and a black leather jacket—was especially popular with gay men themselves.

MAJOR AMERICAN DESIGNERS

By the 1990s, male fashions in both suits and leisurewear were routinely part of the ready-to-wear collections produced by the leading designers at the time. Donna Karan and Tommy Hilfiger were two of the best-known American names whose menswear set trends globally. Donna Karan produced suits that were well cut, restrained, and easy to wear, while Tommy Hilfiger dominated the designer market for casualwear. Hilfiger's designs, anonymous except for their prominent labels, were especially popular with African-American men. The casualwear market was also led by sportswear, and styles worn by the American athletes in the Olympics and the World Athletics Championships were widely copied.

The manufactured pop group the Village People took icons of male American culture—the construction worker, the cowboy, a G.I, a cop, a Native American, and a biker—and transformed them into icons of gay culture.

FLAMBOYANT STYLES

Swedish tennis player Bjorn Borg was an international champion who dominated men's tennis in the 1970s and early 1980s. His rival and successor in the early 1980s was the American John McEnroe, who had beaten him in the Wimbdon men's singles final. During the time that both players were on the international circuit, the fashion was for longer hair, and so both wore headbands to keep their hair in place—and the sweat out of their eyes. They were widely imitated by men on and off the tennis court, reviving the headbands of the hippie days.

In the 1990s, tennis style influenced mainstream clothing and other sports when Andre Agassi, a flamboyant champion from Las Vegas, went on the court in colored Lycra clothing. While Agassi took his fashion lead from other athletes at the time, he was a fashion leader in two other areas: he popularized large wraparound sunglasses that tied around the back of the head, as well as long, close-fitting bicycling shorts that were worn under more traditional, looser tennis shorts.

GOLF CLOTHES

Until the 1920s, golfers had worn knickerbockers: roomy, full pants that finished at the knee, where they were gathered together with straps or buttons. Their full cut meant that they offered the wearer a lot of room, and so would not

The woman's cloche hat and the man's Fair Isle pullover and plus fours were the height of 1920s golf fashion.

affect his or her swing. Furthermore, their short length meant that they did not get in the way of the golfer's attempts at hitting the ball accurately.

Golf was incredibly popular in the 1920s, and once again, the Prince of Wales was a promoter of styles in the United States. An enthusiastic golfer, the Prince started a new fashion when he appeared on the golf course in **plus fours**, a pant style so named because they were gathered in four inches (about 10 cm) below the knee; they were also cut straight and full in the leg. The Prince of Wales wore his plus fours with long, multicolored socks, two-toned shoes, and a bright, checked jacket. A Fair Isle sweater, a pullover, and a large tweed golfing cap completed the look.

THE STYLE OF CHAMPIONS

As in other sports, the clothing worn by the champions of the time was widely imitated. For example, the huge popularity of plus fours in the United States at this time was enhanced by homegrown champions, such as Walter Hagan, who wore them to match-winning success. However, the most influential golfer of this period was Bobby Jones. Over 100 years after his birth, Jones is still the most successful golfer of all time. He won 13 major championships from 1923 to 1930, and he is still the only golfer to have succeeded in wining all four major international golf championships in a single year. In those days, that meant the British Amateur Championship, the British Open, the American Open, and the American Amateur.

From the 1960s onwards, t-shirts and shorts, here worn by surfers in Australia, were too comfortable in warm weather to go out of fashion.

CHAPTER 4

Major Designers

From the 1950s, as men became more interested in fashion, designers explored new styles. The growth of the ready-to-wear market encouraged designers to explore this new territory. Young men were more likely to buy off-the-rack clothes with designer labels than to buy bespoke clothing.

YVES SAINT LAURENT (1950s)

Born in Algeria, Yves Saint Laurent began his career as assistant to the French **couturier** Christian Dior, taking over that fashion house when Dior died in 1957. A radical designer, Saint Laurent provoked alarm within Paris fashion

The flamboyant designer Gianni Versace (right), pictured with Elton John (wearing glasses), helped brighten men's fashion. Male models (right) were popular on the catwalks in the 1990s.

circles with his argument that street fashions should inspire designers, a view that was opposite to the way everyone else thought at the time. He took men's clothes, such as the French workingman's smock, blazer, and overcoat, and redesigned them for women. He also designed suits and separates for men in a distinctive style.

PIERRE CARDIN (1960s)

A Frenchman born in Italy, Pierre Cardin initially made his reputation in the 1950s as a designer of theatrically inspired costumes. In 1957, he opened his first menswear shop, selling ready-to-wear instead of haute couture garments, and he launched his first ready-to-wear menswear collection in 1960.

Cardin upset the French design establishment by producing ready-to wear clothes instead of haute couture designs. His collarless suits, in corduroy or striped cotton, were made famous throughout the world by the rock group The Beatles, who wore them on stage at the insistence of their manager, Brian Epstein. Cardin was the first designer to license his name for use in ready-to-wear collections with a distinctive style. By the end of the century, the Cardin name was licensed for use on over 400 items, from tinned fish to sunglasses.

PACO RABANNE (1960s)

Paco Rabanne was best known in the 1960s for using plastic and other unusual materials to make clothing. Along with Pierre Cardin, he was among the first menswear designers to license his name for use on men's clothing and accessories. His cologne and aftershave lotion were popular throughout the 1960s and 1970s.

NINO CERRUTI (1960S–1980s)

In 1950, Nino Cerruti took over his family's textile firm, but it was not until 1967 that he launched his first menswear collection and became a leading

ICONIC UNDERPANTS

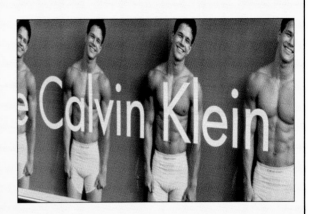

Calvin Klein underpants were among the biggest selling items of underwear during the 1980s. Among some men—usually younger ones—it was fashionable to wear them so that the name "Calvin Klein," which appeared on the waistband, peeked out above their pants. So commonplace was this undergarment that it even entered the Hollywood lexicon. In the film *Back to the Future*, made in 1985, the main character Marty McFly, played by Michael J. Fox, travels back in time and meets a character that calls him Calvin Klein because that is the name written on his boxer shorts. In the early 1990s, Klein unveiled a unisex range of underpants that enjoyed great success, thanks to an advertisement campaign featuring black and white photos of the model Kate Moss and the singer/actor Mark Wahlberg.

menswear designer. Cerruti suits were typical of the 1980s "power dressing" style, referring to the vogue for stylish suits with vests; these outfits were supposed to represent the image of the hard-nosed executive.

CALVIN KLEIN (1970s)

After working for various coat and suit manufacturers, Calvin Klein began his own business designing coats and suits in 1968. In the 1970s, he and Ralph Lauren (separately) revived the "college" look of a grey flannel suit with a loose waisted jacket and narrow shoulders, named after the style worn on Ivy League university campuses. His name was subsequently seen on menswear, including sportswear and casual clothing, but he became well-known for his "designer jeans." Launched in 1978, this style was cut to fit a fuller frame and was more expensive than the traditional Levis brand. Shortly afterward, the Calvin Klein logo was on a huge range of clothing and accessories, including unisex perfume.

Today, Calvin Klein remains a major fashion force. The typical Calvin Klein look includes chinos in soft, dull colors, turtleneck sweaters, and blazers made from expensive fabrics and natural, soft materials, such as linen, wool, and silk. Klein also designs unisexwear and womenswear that, like his menswear, typically follows a simple, pared-down style.

RALPH LAUREN (1970s)

Another American designer to have successfully created a lifestyle associated with a brand name, Lauren began his career working for the Brooks Brothers menswear store while also working as a glove salesman. In 1967, he began designing for Beau Brummell Neckwear, and he set up the "Polo" branch of the company, initially to make handmade ties. He went on to launch his own label in 1972, and he became internationally famous for his work as the costume designer on the 1974 film *The Great Gatsby*.

Throughout his designing career, Lauren has often revived the styles of previous decades in American history. Today, the "Polo" logo, an image of a polo player, is associated with the Ralph Lauren name on all kinds of menswear, especially the Polo casual shirt.

GIORGIO ARMANI (1980s)

The Armani name initially became internationally known as the leading designer of the unstructured suit, popular in the early 1980s. Armani took away padding, linings, and various other aspects of a suit's design that stiffened and shaped it. His approach was especially suited to the production techniques of the Italian tailoring industry.

Hollywood and television stars promoted Armani designs throughout the 1980s. Richard Gere, for example, wore Armani suits in the popular 1980 film *American Gigolo.* Armani continued to influence men's fashion for the rest of the century, and today, his clothes are still considered stylish and classic.

DONNA KARAN (1980s)

Donna Karan's first designs were in sportswear, but she became internationally known in the 1980s for designing well-cut, practical clothes of all kinds. Karan typically uses luxurious fabrics, such as cashmere or wool, to make men's suits and separates in soft, dark colors. Her label, "Donna Karan," and its sportier variation, "DKNY" (Donna Karan New York), are available internationally.

GIANNI VERSACE (1990s)

The leading Italian designer after Armani, Gianni Versace began his career working in leather and suede before he started his own fashion label in 1978. Like his popular womenswear, Versace's menswear was often brightly colored and extravagant, characteristics appealing to men who wanted something louder than the typical restrained, traditional American designs. Versace's designs for men included stretchy, multicolored, one-piece suits reminiscent of those racing cyclists wore.

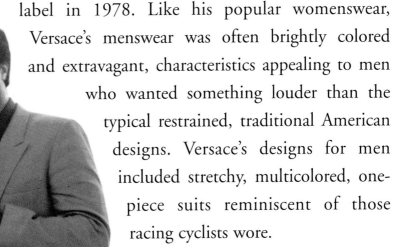

Crockett and Tubbs, played by Don Johnson (left) and Phillip Michael Thomas (right), were the cool, Armani-clad detectives in the 1980s police drama *Miami Vice.*

GLOSSARY

Checks square patterns usually based on lines of contrasting colors

Chino a usually khaki cotton or synthetic-fiber twill of the type used for military uniforms

Couturier an establishment engaged in the business of designing, making, and selling fashionable custom-made clothing

Cravat a band or scarf worn around the neck

Double-breasted one half of the front lapping over the other, usually with a double row of buttons and a single row of buttonholes

Fair Isle a style of knitting originating in the Shetland Islands that is characterized by bands of multicolored geometric patterns

Haute couture the houses or designers that create exclusive and often trend-setting fashions

Hedonistic relating to a belief that pleasure or happiness is the sole or chief good in life

Homburg hat a man's felt hat with a stiff curled brim and a high crown creased lengthwise

Jersey a plain weft-knitted fabric made of wool, cotton, nylon, rayon, or silk

Knickerbockers full, loose pants that are gathered below the knee with straps and a buckle. Typically worn for golf, shooting, and other sporting activities at the turn of the century

Long johns long underwear

Manifesto a written statement declaring publicly the intentions, motives, or views of its issuer

Morning suit men's daytime dress for formal occasions; usually consists of a winged-collar shirt, vest, sportsjacket or blazer, and formal trousers

Oxford bags straight-cut baggy pants with wide legs

Panama hat a lightweight hat of natural-colored straw

Plus fours long, wide, men's knickerbockers usually worn for golf; so-named because the overhang at the knee requires an extra four inches (10 cm) of material

Pogrom an organized massacre of helpless people, specifically, the Jews

Porkpie hat a hat with a low telescoped crown, flat top, and brim turned up all around or up in back and down in front

Quiff a prominent lock of hair over the forehead

Seersucker a lightweight, crinkled fabric made by weaving together fibers that shrink at different rates

Single-breasted having a center closing with one row of buttons and no lapel

Spats a cloth or leather gaiter covering the instep and ankle

Taffeta a crisp, plain-woven, lustrous fabric of various fibers

Tank top a sleeveless, collarless shirt with usually wide shoulder straps and no front opening

Tweed a rough, woolen fabric

Tyrolean hat a hat of a style originating in the Tirol and marked by soft, often green, felt, a narrow brim, and pointed crown, and adorned with an ornamental feather

TIMELINE

1900 Middle-class men adopt the three-piece suit.

1914–1918 Relatively unaffected by World War I, the U.S. emerges for the first time as a fashion trendsetter.

1925 F. Scott Fitzgerald publishes *The Great Gatsby*, and the character of Jay Gatsby becomes the male role model of the 1920s.

1931 Warner Brothers gangster films, such as *Enemies of the Public* and *Shame of A Nation*, make stars of James Cagney and Paul Muni; young men copy their double-breasted suits with their wide, trendy lapels.

1936 The first pairs of Bass Weejuns, the original loafers, are sold.

1950s American fashion spreads in popularity throughout Europe, especially among teenagers.

1952 The polo shirt, based on Rene Lacoste's tennis shirt, goes on sale in the U.S.

1960s "Swinging London" is the center of fashion, and men's ready-to-wear clothes become more fashionable than the traditional bespoke style.

1967 The "Summer of Love" represents the height of counterculture and hippie fashions.

1970s Glam rock sets fashion trends.

1973 The oil crisis causes a global economic collapse; secondhand clothes and the styles of the 1930s and 1940s become popular.

1980s An economic revival creates the yuppie; typically employed in the financial sector, yuppies dress in three-piece suits and striped shirts with white collars and cuffs.

1990s All of the major fashion labels are producing ranges of clothing and accessories for men.

FURTHER INFORMATION

BOOKS

Bolton, Andrew. *Men in Skirts*. New York: V & A Publications, 2002.

Bond, David. *The Guinness Guide to Twentieth-Century Fashion*. Enfield: Guinness Superlatives Limited, 1981.

Brush Kidwell, Claudia and Valerie Steele. *Men and Women: Dressing the Part*. Washington: Smithsonian Institution Press, 1989.

Chenoune, Farid. *A History of Men's Fashion*. Paris: Flammarion, 1993.

Costantino, Maria. *Men's Fashion in the 20th Century*. London: Batsford, 1997.

Flusser, Alan. *Style and the Man*. New York: Harper Collins, 1996.

Flusser, Alan. *Dressing the Man: The Art of Permanent Fashion*. New York: Harper Collins, 2002.

Harris, Carol. *Miller's Collecting Twentieth-Century Fashion and Accessories*. London: Mitchell Beazley, 2000.

Johnson Gross, Kim, Woody Hockswender, and David Bashaw. *Men's Wardrobe (Chic Simple)*. Westminster: Knopf, 1998.

Omelianuk, Scott and Ted Allen. *Esquire's Things a Man Should Know About Style*. New York: Esquire, 1999.

Peacock, John. *Men's Fashion*. London: Thames and Hudson, 2000.

Polhemus, Ted. *Streetstyle*. London: Thames and Hudson, 1994.

Watt, Judith (ed.). *The Penguin Book of Twentieth-Century Fashion Writing*. London: Viking, 1999.

Wilson, Elizabeth and Lou Taylor. *Through the Looking Glass*. London: BBC Books, 1996.

ONLINE SOURCES

The Costume Gallery

www.costumegallery.com

Research 20th-century fashions with this site, which specializes in pictures and information on changing fashions throughout the decades.

Costume Society of America

www.costumesocietyamerica.com

The Costume Society of America is a national organization devoted to all aspects of costume and fashion, both modern and historical. The site gives details of local and national C.S.A. events, including exhibitions and courses, and has an extensive online bookshop.

Southern Californian Lindy Society

www.lindyhopping.com/fashionhistm.html

Detailed history of men's fashions in the 1920s, and extensive information and links about lindy hopping.

Men's Fashion Magazines

www.gq-magazine.co.uk

www.esquire.com

These Web sites feature the latest in men's fashions. The first is the site for the British-based magazine, *GQ*, and the second is for *Esquire* magazine, an American publication.

ABOUT THE AUTHORS

Mike Brown lives in London, England, where he writes part-time and teaches part-time, in addition to giving talks and lectures on 20th-century history and architecture to a wide range of audiences, from primary schools to retirement groups. He has written a book on Britain's Civil Defence Services in World War II, *Put That Light Out* (Sutton, 1999), *A Child's War* (Sutton, 2000), and, in conjunction with his wife, Carol Harris, *The Wartime House* (Sutton, 2000).

Carol Harris is a freelance journalist and lecturer specializing in the 1920s, 1930s, and 1940s. She has contributed to exhibitions at the Imperial War Museum on wartime fashions and utility clothing, and she regularly gives talks on these topics. Her other books include *Collecting Twentieth-Century Fashion and Accessories* (Mitchell Beazley, 1999), and *Women at War—the Home Front* (Sutton, 2001).

INDEX